LANDSLIDES AND AVALANCHES

PHOTO CREDITS

Front Cover & 1 - Andrei Kovin, 2 - Lysogor Roman, 4 - Lucky Team Studio, A_Lesik, 5 - Roel Slootweg, PK289, 6 - fabiodevilla, eWilding, 7 - Elena Larina, Photobac, 8 - Ingo Menhard, think4photop, Christopher Boswell, 9 - blew_s, 10 - Nick Hawkes, Troutnut, 11 - Ekaterina Kolomeets, Josef Hanus, 12 - Lucky Team Studio, Marco Maggesi, 13 - mTaira, 14 - Lucky Team Studio, 15 - castate, Harald Schmidt, 16 - Sashkin, Kirill Volkov, Alexlky, 17 - Bannafarsai_Stock, Geet Theerawat, 18 - Giongi63, Northfoto, Pyty, Fenton one, 19 - United States Geological Survey, Edu Alarcon, AVM, 20 - Jag_cz, Lysogor Roman, 21 - eWilding, Forge Photography, 22 - Kotenko Oleksandr, Fedor Selivanov, 23 - Everett Historical, Landscape Nature Photo, 24 - moreimages, Ovchinnikova Irina, 25 - ErichFend, Jakob Kennedy, 26 - Belish, PlusONE, 27 - Dmytro Vietrov, Brian Finestone, 28 - Naeblys, peiyang, Vitalii Matokha, 29 - Christian Bickel fingalo, 30 - Cascade Creatives, RonGreer.Com.
Images are courtesy of Shutterstock.com. With thanks to Getty Images, Thinkstock Photo and iStockphoto.

BookLife
PUBLISHING

©2018
BookLife Publishing
King's Lynn
Norfolk PE30 4LS

A catalogue record for this book is available from the British Library.

ISBN: 978-1-78637-502-5

Written by:
Joanna Brundle

Edited by:
Kirsty Holmes

Designed by:
Gareth Liddington

LANDSLIDES AND AVALANCHES

CONTENTS

Words that look like **this** can be found in the glossary on page 31.

WHAT IS A LANDSLIDE?

Do you ever think about the ground underneath your feet? It feels solid and still, doesn't it? But imagine how terrifying it would be if you were to see the ground moving, sliding and slipping away.

A landslide is exactly what it sounds like – a mass of soil, rock, **debris**, vegetation or mud sliding down a slope. These materials are pulled downhill by the force of **gravity** and move by slipping, falling or flowing.

Landslides can cause serious damage.

Every year, landslides claim the lives of thousands of people all around the world.

Landslides also happen under the sea and on other planets, including Mars and Venus.

The collapse of part of a hillside caused this large landslide in Rwanda.

Landslides sometimes happen very slowly and gradually, although some can be very fast-moving. The slowest landslides creep at less than one centimetre (cm) a year. Fast-moving landslides typically travel at around five metres (m) per second. They happen suddenly and with little warning. They are also very dangerous because people in their path do not have time to escape. The more land that moves, the more serious the effects of the landslide.

You may have seen small landslides at the side of the road in hilly or mountainous areas.

WHAT CAUSES LANDSLIDES?

Landslides happen when the force of gravity acting down a slope is greater than the forces holding the slope materials together. The most important force holding together the **bedrock** and the material on top is **friction**. Landslides occur when something happens to interfere with this friction.

RAINFALL

Heavy rain is often the trigger for a landslide. A storm or a long period of wet weather may cause the ground to become **saturated**. Rainwater and **meltwater** reduce the friction between the bedrock and material on the surface.

The extra weight of storm rains or meltwater can also cause previous landslides to move again.

In spring, water from melting snow and ice can trigger a landslide in hilly or mountainous areas.

WEATHERING

Weathering is the breaking up of rocks due to the action of the weather. Rainwater enters cracks in rocks and expands as it freezes. This process, called freeze-thaw, makes the cracks larger. As the water thaws and refreezes, the rock is weakened and may break off, triggering a landslide.

These cliffs are gradually being eroded by the waves and are falling into the sea.

EROSION

The gradual wearing away of weathered rock is called erosion. When erosion happens on a mountain or at the base of cliffs, it can leave overhanging rock. The overhanging rock eventually breaks off, causing a landslide. Rivers, streams, glaciers and waves all cause erosion.

Overhanging Rocks

EARTHQUAKES

Earthquakes violently tilt layers of rock beneath the ground. They release energy in the form of shock waves that vibrate the ground on and below the surface. These movements can trigger a landslide.

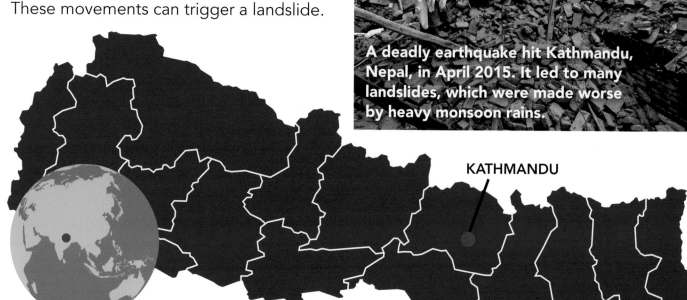

A deadly earthquake hit Kathmandu, Nepal, in April 2015. It led to many landslides, which were made worse by heavy monsoon rains.

KATHMANDU

VOLCANIC ACTIVITY

The energy released by an erupting volcano can trigger a landslide on the mountainside. An erupting volcano also spews out molten rock called lava and other materials. A pyroclastic flow is a boiling-hot mass of volcanic rock, ash and gas that races down the side of an erupting volcano. Lahars are a type of mudslide that form when water – either from heavy rain or snow melted by pyroclastic flow – mixes with volcanic ash and dust.

These ridges in Washington, USA, were formed by ancient lahar mudslides.

HUMAN CAUSES OF LANDSLIDES

Mining and quarrying can cause landslides by making the ground less stable. Poor construction of buildings, roads, dams and canals can have the same effect. **Wildfires**, which usually start because of human activities, remove trees and other vegetation that holds soil together. **Deforestation** can cause landslides for the same reason.

Deforestation on a slope increases the chances of a landslide happening.

A huge landslide in Bangladesh in 2017 killed over 150 people. It was triggered by heavy rain, but deforestation of hill slopes made the problem worse. Villagers who could not afford to buy more expensive land in safer areas had been forced to build their homes on slopes where

Around 30% of the world's landslides happen in a mountainous region of Asia, called the Himalayas. A combination of steep mountain slopes, high rainfall, earthquakes and human action is responsible.

DIFFERENT TYPES OF LANDSLIDE

CREEP

Creep happens when soil moves very slowly down a gentle slope. It may be caused by freeze-thaw weathering or by non-stop wetting and drying of the soil. It usually happens so slowly that scientific equipment may be needed to detect it.

A different type of creep happens in areas of permafrost – where the ground under the surface is permanently frozen. When the surface layer thaws in summer, the meltwater cannot soak away through the permafrost. The wet, heavy soil sticks together, forming a large mass that moves slowly downhill, until the next freeze.

Land with underlying permafrost is called tundra. Tundra is a type of biome.

SLUMPS AND FALLS

Slumps happen occasionally but rapidly when curved slabs of earth or rock fall away from a slope. Terraces – or large steps – are left behind. Falls happen when rock or other materials plummet through the air at speed. Rockfalls are the most common type of fall. Ground shaking caused by earthquakes is a common trigger for rockfalls. In mountain areas, rockfalls are particularly common in spring, triggered by meltwater. Over time, rockfalls build up at the base of cliffs or mountains, forming a slope called a talus slope.

Large slabs of rock break into small, rough chunks when they hit the ground.

Talus Slope

Turtle Mountain, Rocky Mountains, Canada

In 1903, a huge rockslide fell from Turtle Mountain onto the mining town of Frank, killing 80 people. Over a century later, the effects are still visible.

FLOWS AND SLIDES

Mudslides can bury roads and even cars.

Flows are a mixture of water, rock and **sediment**. They move rapidly downhill and may block roads and rivers. Large flows can bury entire villages. Slides happen when a section of rock or soil suddenly breaks away from the side of a slope and moves quickly downhill as one mass of material. Unlike falls, both flows and slides stay in contact with the surface of the ground. Storms with heavy rainfall may cause mudslides that bury everything in their path. Flows and slides into river valleys may block the river causing flooding **upstream**.

In 2010, a huge landslide in Northern Pakistan blocked the River Hunza. This formed a lake behind the blockage that flooded farmland and caused 30,000 people to be evacuated from submerged villages.

This is an aerial view of a landslide in the Italian Alps.

SUBMARINE LANDSLIDES

Landslides that happen underneath the ocean are called submarine landslides. They are often caused by underwater earthquakes or volcanic eruptions. A rapidly-moving submarine landslide may cause so much water to be **displaced** that a tsunami is caused. A tsunami is a series of waves that race outwards across the ocean at speeds up to 800 kilometres per hour (kph). As they reach land, the waves slow down but gain height. The huge waves crash onto the coast, causing flooding and devastation. Tsunamis can also be caused by landslides falling into the sea in coastal areas.

Tsunamis cause devastating damage.

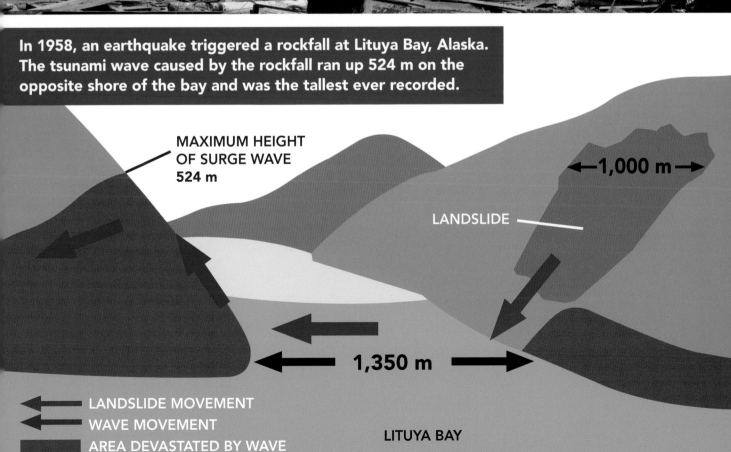

In 1958, an earthquake triggered a rockfall at Lituya Bay, Alaska. The tsunami wave caused by the rockfall ran up 524 m on the opposite shore of the bay and was the tallest ever recorded.

MAXIMUM HEIGHT OF SURGE WAVE
524 m

←1,000 m→

LANDSLIDE

←1,350 m→

LANDSLIDE MOVEMENT
WAVE MOVEMENT
AREA DEVASTATED BY WAVE

LITUYA BAY

Landslides can cause injury and death. They also damage property, including cars, homes and businesses.

EFFECTS OF LANDSLIDES

The effects of natural disasters such as landslides are often worse in less economically developed countries (**LEDCs**), where people have few **resources**. A lack of safe building land may have forced them to build their homes in places at risk from landslides or where landslides have happened previously. LEDCs may lack proper drainage for heavy rains. Early warning systems that give people in danger time to evacuate their homes may not be in place.

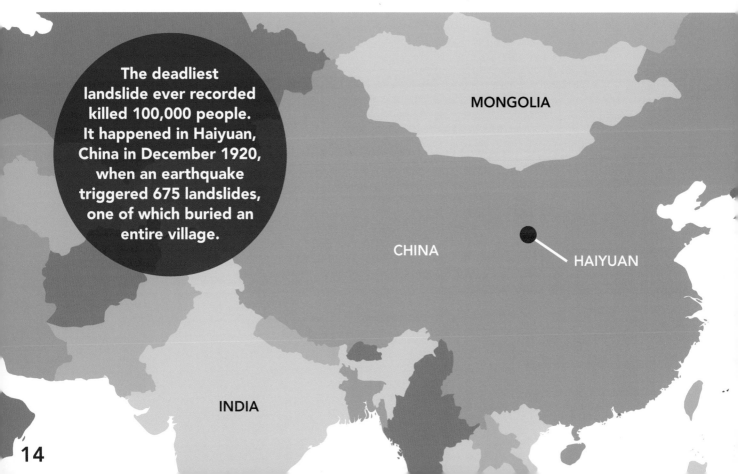

The deadliest landslide ever recorded killed 100,000 people. It happened in Haiyuan, China in December 1920, when an earthquake triggered 675 landslides, one of which buried an entire village.

MONGOLIA

CHINA

HAIYUAN

INDIA

Landslides may damage communication and transport systems, including road and rail networks and bridges. Essential services, such as electricity and water supplies and sewage systems, may be affected. All of these problems make it harder for people to live and to earn money. **Tourism**, an important source of income, may suffer. Many years after a landslide, the appearance of an area can still be badly affected. As well as the cost in human lives, it is also very expensive to repair the damage caused by landslides and to provide medical care for the injured.

This huge mudslide in the Austrian Alps has blocked a mountain stream.

This beach in California, USA, is littered with debris from mudslides that happened in 2018.

The mudslides in California were triggered by wildfires, followed by heavy rain.

PREDICTING, PREVENTING AND SURVIVING LANDSLIDES

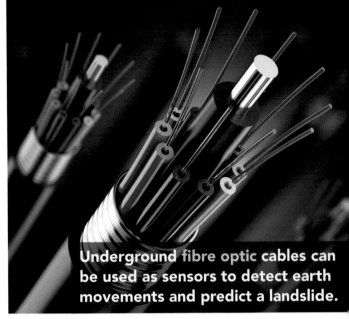

Underground fibre optic cables can be used as sensors to detect earth movements and predict a landslide.

Landslides are particularly dangerous when they happen without warning, but scientists are developing new ways to predict them. They look at the steepness of a slope, the type of rock, whether the land is wooded or open and the position of homes and roads. This information is combined with detailed weather forecasts and earthquake predictions to understand when and where landslides may happen.

Doors and windows suddenly jamming in their frames or the appearance of new cracks in driveways and walls can be signs that the ground is moving and that a landslide is possible.

This can lead to this.

Humans cannot prevent the natural causes of landslides such as earthquakes and rainfall. We can, however, help to prevent landslide damage by limiting activities such as building, mining and deforestation in areas where landslides are likely.

Building protective barriers helps to contain rockfalls.

Replanting slopes with trees and other vegetation gives some protection against landslides.

If you are caught in a landslide, try to move sideways, out of its path.

Evacuate your home immediately if told to do so.

If you cannot get out of the way, roll into a ball and cover your head with your arms.

Never try to outrun a landslide – they move much faster than we can run.

VARGAS, VENEZUELA, 1999

Venezuela lies in the north of South America, bordering the Caribbean Sea. In December 1999, the country suffered the worst natural disaster in its history. Two weeks of torrential rain had fallen on the mountainous regions of the country. Deadly landslides composed of boulders, debris, water and mud followed. The state of Vargas and other northern areas of the country were devastated. A 100 km stretch of coastline was destroyed. Many people were buried under the mud or washed out to sea.

Chavez was criticised for failing to evacuate people before the tragedy struck.

Hugo Chavez, President of Venezuela in 1999

CARIBBEAN SEA

VENEZUELA

SOUTH AMERICA

This is an area called the Caraballeda fan. The deposits of rock and earth are up to six metres deep. In total, about 1.8 million cubic metres of boulders and other materials were dumped in this area.

Many houses were destroyed in the landslide.

The narrow coastal strip between the mountains and the sea was very densely populated. As a result, many people died – between 10,000 and 30,000. Many more were made homeless. The coastal town of Los Corales was completely buried under three metres of mud. Throughout the area, public services such as water, electricity and telephone lines were wiped out. An estimated 190,000 people had to be evacuated. People with the lowest incomes and fewest resources suffered the most. Their rickety homes were swept away into the sea by the mudslides and floods.

The cost of the damage was estimated to be over three billion dollars.

Landslides can damage the base of buildings as the mud and rocks collide with the bottom floors. This can lead to high-rise buildings, like this one, collapsing.

WHAT IS AN AVALANCHE?

An avalanche can travel more quickly than the fastest skier, reaching speeds up to 130 kph within a few seconds.

It can be great fun to spend time in the mountains skiing, snowboarding or sledging. The beautiful, snow-covered slopes look harmless, but there is always a risk of an avalanche. An avalanche is a mass of snow and ice that rushes down a mountain. Avalanches happen when an unstable mass of snow breaks away from the mountainside and slides downhill. As it moves downhill, an avalanche speeds up, throwing up a cloud of ice particles high above the moving stream of snow.

The term avalanche is sometimes also used to refer to rock and soil landslides. Snow avalanches are sometimes called snow slides.

Avalanches happen in mountainous regions all over the world. Depending on where they happen, they may not cause any damage but, because of their speed and force, they bury everything in their path, including people. Avalanches are the greatest danger to human life in mountainous areas and around 150 people are killed by them every year. In some places, the authorities monitor the risk of avalanches and warn mountain users of the dangers. They may set off small explosions to trigger small, controlled avalanches when nobody is present.

Warning signs advise people on the mountain of the avalanche risk.

NO SKIING!
AVALANCHE DANGER SLOPE!

In 2018, a group of villages in the French Alps called Tignes recorded the heaviest snowfalls in 20 years. Because of this, they raised the avalanche risk to level 5 (very high).

WHAT CAUSES AVALANCHES?

Repeated falls of snow on a mountainside build up layers called the snowpack. Cutting down into the snowpack reveals layers of snow that vary in thickness and texture. The layers may be firmly joined together but, if the bonds are weak, a layer may break away, causing an avalanche. A new, powdery snowfall, for example, may form only a weak bond with a smooth, icy surface underneath. It may then fall away, like snow sliding down a car windscreen.

Heavy snowstorms are the main cause of avalanches. Most happen within 24 hours of a snowstorm that drops 30 cm or more of fresh snow.

Avalanches can happen whenever the downhill force of gravity is stronger than the force of the bonds holding the snow layers together.

Meltwater and rainfall can also make the snowpack unstable and trigger an avalanche.

Strong winds can blow snow into an overhanging ledge called a cornice. The weight of the snow eventually causes the ledge to break off.

Vibrations from natural events such as thunder, lightning, earthquakes or volcanic eruptions can start avalanches, by dislodging unstable snow layers. Many human activities are also the cause.

Vibrations from gunshots, explosives, loud machinery, construction and winter sport activities can all trigger avalanches. Deforestation and soil erosion in mountain areas also make the snowpack less stable.

During World War I, avalanches killed 60,000 soldiers who were fighting in the Alps. The avalanches were thought to have been triggered by gunfire.

TYPICAL AVALANCHE SLOPES

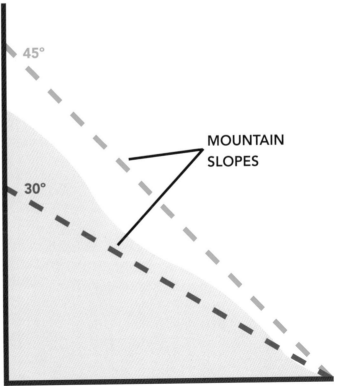

45°

MOUNTAIN SLOPES

30°

Most avalanches happen on mountain slopes with an angle between 30 and 45 degrees.

DIFFERENT TYPES OF AVALANCHE

POWDER AVALANCHES

Powder avalanches are slides of dry, powdery snow. They often form when heavy snow falls on a slippery layer beneath, for example after rain or frost. This forms a weak layer at the top of the snowpack. Powder avalanches start from a single point, picking up more snow and spreading outwards in a fan shape as they travel downhill.

Fan-Shaped Avalanche

A Powder Avalanche in the Himalayas

As the core of snow rushes downhill, it kicks up a powdery cloud of snow and air. A powerful **vortex** forms at the front of the avalanche, powerful enough to rip up trees and small buildings.

Powder avalanches can reach speeds of up to 300 kph on very steep slopes.

Wet avalanches happen during the spring thaw, when meltwater trickles through the snowpack, saturating weak layers of snow. Eventually, these layers cannot support the weight of the water and they break away.

SLAB AVALANCHES

Slab avalanches happen where a weak layer in the snowpack is covered by compressed layers of snow. If an avalanche is triggered, the weak underneath layer breaks away downhill, taking the top layers with it. The whole mass falls down the mountainside at high speed as a giant slab, breaking into smaller chunks as it continues its journey. Slab avalanches pose a deadly threat to people on the mountain, such as skiers and mountaineers, because of their speed and the size of the slab.

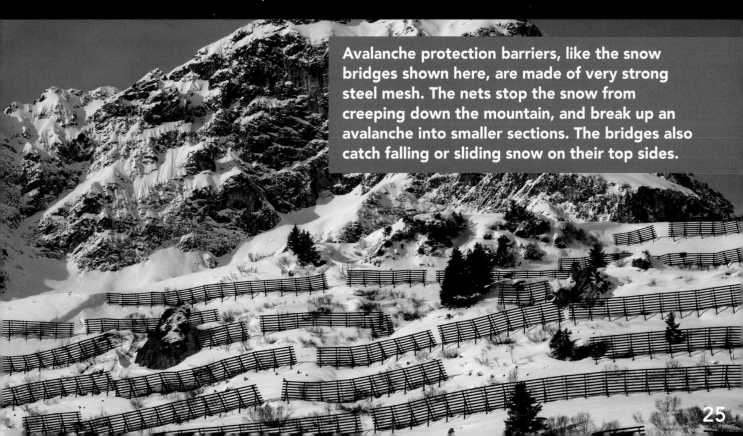

Avalanche protection barriers, like the snow bridges shown here, are made of very strong steel mesh. The nets stop the snow from creeping down the mountain, and break up an avalanche into smaller sections. The bridges also catch falling or sliding snow on their top sides.

SURVIVING AN AVALANCHE

People who are buried in an avalanche need to be rescued quickly if they are to survive. If help comes within 15 minutes, over 90% survive. Specially trained rescue teams help people who have been caught in an avalanche. Dogs show rescuers where to dig.

If you see or hear an avalanche coming, you should ski or board straight downhill as fast as you can and then try to move to the side to get out of the path of the avalanche. Try to grab a tree to save yourself from being tossed around.

Always ski or board with an adult. Follow avalanche warnings and stick to marked runs rather than going 'off piste'.

A team of rescuers are digging for survivors after an avalanche.

Rescue dogs are able to locate the scent of a survivor trapped under two metres of snow.

It is important to have the right equipment with you when you are having fun in the mountains. It can save your life or help you to rescue someone else if an avalanche should happen. An inflatable air bag could provide life-saving air for someone who is buried, while help is coming. A folding shovel is essential for digging. Probes, used for pinpointing buried survivors, are lightweight metal tubes that fold up. A transceiver can send and receive radio signals to guide rescuers to you or help you to locate someone else.

AVALANCHE RESCUE KIT

TRANSCEIVER

PROBES

FOLDING SHOVEL

Helicopters are used to rescue survivors from remote areas of the mountain.

FLATEYRI, ICELAND, 1995

Flateyri is backed by Mount Skollahvilft. Avalanches in the area are common. Residents had tried to protect themselves by building their homes away from the avalanche danger zone and away from paths that avalanches had taken in the past. In October 1995, an avalanche warning was issued, following heavy snowfalls. People living near the avalanche danger zone at the base of the mountain were evacuated. On the 26th of October, a 3.7 metre-high slab broke away from the mountainside and hurtled downhill at speeds up to 200 kph.

FLATEYRI

ICELAND

Flateyri is a fishing village in Iceland, around 50 km from the Arctic Circle.

Flateyri

The avalanche followed an unexpected path, bypassing evacuated homes. Over 250,000 tonnes (t) of snow came to rest in the centre of the village. Residents were asleep when the avalanche struck at 4am, so they were unaware of the danger and had no time to escape. They awoke to the deafening roar of a 500-metre-wide avalanche of ice, snow and rocks.

In 1998, an A-shaped protection structure, called an avalanche dam, was built up the mountainside.

The dam was put to the test when two large avalanches struck in February 1999 and March 2000. Each time, the dam safely directed the avalanches into the sea and the village was saved.

The dam deflects avalanches away from the village.

WELLINGTON, USA, 1910

Wellington, Washington State, USA, was the scene of the worst avalanche disaster in the USA to date. On the 1st of March 1910, two trains, trapped in the Cascade Mountains due to days of snow storms, were swept away by the avalanche. They fell 45 m down into a steep valley. The disaster, which killed 96 people, was triggered by thunder and lightning. Previous deforestation and forest fires on the mountainside worsened the effects of the avalanche by clearing a path for it above the railway tracks. The fires had been started by sparks from the passing steam trains.

This is Stevens Pass, Washington, USA, the scene of the worst avalanche disaster in the history of the USA.

Debris from the crashed trains can still be seen in the valley today.

GLOSSARY

bedrock	the lower layer of the Earth's crust, made of solid rock
biome	a community of plant and animal life, adapted to the conditions in which it lives, or the type of region in which this community lives, for example tundra, forests and deserts
compressed	pressed together
debris	loose fragments of rock or other materials
deforestation	the cutting down and removal of trees in a forest to provide timber or space for farming or building
displaced	move something from its usual place
evacuated	moved away from an area to escape danger
fibre optic	very thin strands of glass arranged in bundles and used to send digital information
friction	the force that tries to stop objects in contact with one another from moving
glaciers	slow-moving masses of thick ice
gravity	the force that pulls everything down towards the centre of the Earth
LEDCs	countries with poor living standards and little industry that are trying to become more advanced
meltwater	water that has come from melting snow and ice, particularly a glacier
resources	useful things such as money, equipment and materials
saturated	completely soaked with moisture
sediment	small pieces of rock, minerals and animal and plant remains
submerged	completely under water
tourism	the action of visiting new places for pleasure and the industry that supports this action
upstream	towards the source of a river, against the flow of water
vortex	a swirling mass of water or air
wildfires	large, destructive fires that burn in an area of vegetation such as woodland, bushes or grasses

INDEX